HAGIA SOPHIA

HAGIA SOPHIA

Archaeologist
İlhan Akşit

akşit
AKŞIT KÜLTÜR VE TURİZM YAYINCILIK

Edited by

AKŞİT KÜLTÜR ve TURİZM YAYINCILIK

■ ■ ■

Written by

İlhan Akşit

■ ■ ■

Translated by

Sylvia Zeybekoğlu

■ ■ ■

Graphic Composition

Zafer Emecan

■ ■ ■

Typesetting

Gülcan Lazım

■ ■ ■

Photos

Tahsin Aydoğmuş

Kadir Kır

Vasken Değirmentaş

Erdal Yazıcı

■ ■ ■

Colour Separation

Figür Grafik

■ ■ ■

Printed by

Seçil Ofset 0212 629 06 15

■ ■ ■

Akşit Kültür ve Turizm Yayıncılık,

Cağaloğlu Yokuşu Cemal Nadir Sokak

Nur İş Hanı 2/4 Cağaloğlu

34440-ISTANBUL / TURKEY

Tel: (+90 212) 511 53 85 – 511 67 82

Fax: (+90 212) 527 68 13

■ ■ ■

Internet: www.aksityayincilik.com.tr

e-mail: aksit@aksityayincilik.com.tr

■ ■ ■

Copyright:

Akşit Kültür ve Turizm Yayıncılık © 2008

ISBN 975-7039-07-1

Contents

reface

Hagia Sophia, one of the most exciting works of art in the course of art history, was first built in 360, during the era of Constantine. Built in the form of a basilica, it was burned down during a rebellion in 404. While it was rebuilt in 415, the new building was not to last very long. On the night of January 13th, 532 it was once again razed by fire during the Nike rebellion. As soon as the emperor had crushed the rebellion, he decided to have a new church built.

When Emperor Justinius declared at the opening of the new Hagia Sophia that had been reconstructed during 532-537, "I have exceeded you, Süleyman," he would never have been able to guess that it would have remained standing for so many years or that it would become one of the greatest monuments in the history of civilization.

During the period of Iconoclasm (726-842), referred to as such because of the antipathy shown towards shown at that time towards pictures, the mosaics in Hagia Sophia were scrapped away and replaced by figures of crosses. The mosaics we see today began to decorate the church once Iconoclasm ended in 842.

Given the change in eras, Hagia Sophia was transformed into a mosque in 1453. It gained new life with the reinforcements and repairs made to it. In contrast to the period of Iconoclasm, the mosaics were covered with a whitewash during the Ottoman era – a practice which protected them. The way the Ottomans treated the mosaics made it possible for them to survive until the present.

After having described the construction and architecture of Hagia Sophia in our book, we devoted a separate section to a tour of the mosaics found inside. Moreover, by accounting for the Islamic elements and structures of the Ottoman period, we have tried to explain how the building forms a 1500-year whole. Hoping that we will be of assistance in getting you to learn something about this magnificent edifice, we leave you one-to-one with Hagia Sophia.

Archaeologist
İlhan Akşit

A Brief History of the Construction of Saint Sophia

After the proclamation of Christianity as the official state religion by Emperor Constantine I, known as "the Great" (324-337 A.D.), the construction of large churches began everywhere in Byzantium. It was primarily because of the tolerance shown by Constantine the Great that he became known as the founder of these churches.

Socrates (380-440), the chronicler of the church history of the period, claims that it was Constantine the Great who first built Hagia (also known as "Saint" or "Aya") Sophia.

One of the world's most outstanding monuments, Hagia Sophia was originally called a Megalo Ecclesia (meaning, a "colossal church"). It was with the fifth century that it began to be called "Sophia." Contrary to what one may think, however, this architectural marvel was not dedicated to a Hagia ("saint"), but rather to the Holy Wisdom (Theia Sophia), which is the second element of the Christian Trinity. Even so, the people of Byzantium continued to call this church the Megalo Ecclesia for a long time. It was with the conquest of Byzantium in 1453 that the name Hagia Sophia came to be used, a practice that continued over the centuries.

The first church was inaugurated with pomp and circumstance on February 15, 360 A.D. Like contemporary religious edifices of the time, it was built with a wooden roof on an oblong basilica.

For a long time, Hagia John Chrysostom, the Patriarch of Constantinople (Istanbul), was embroiled in an on-going conflict with the Empress Eudoxia, wife of Emperor Arcadius (395-408). The Patriarch was sent into exile on June 20, 404 as a result of a dispute over a silver-plated statue of the empress to be

A detail of two hunters on a tiger hunt. Büyük Saray (Great Palace) Museum of Mosaics.

A floor mosaic of the Büyük Saray depicting a tiger ripping apart a deer. Büyük Saray Museum of Mosaics

Camel Jockey Mosaic. *Büyük Saray Museum of Mosaics*
A view of Hagia Sophia.

erected just outside the church. During the riots that immediately followed, the church was partly burned down. Its restoration was completed during the reign of Emperor Theodosius II (408-450). After a long period of restoration, the church was once again inaugurated on October 10, 415. This newly restored Hagia Sophia was to stand intact for slightly more than a century.

Just prior to the sixth century, during the rule of Emperor Justinian the Great (527-565), an intense feud broke out in Byzantium between the Blues and the Greens. Initially, these groups were sports clubs, so-named because they bore those colors when participating in the horse races at the Hippodrome. Later they acquired political identities and began to be transformed into means through which the different political orientations of the people were reflected. In time, the Blues came to stand for Orthodoxy and the large landowners, while the Greens, on the other hand, came to represent the Monophysites, tradesmen and artisans. The ranks in the political, social and religious strata of society thus became clearly distinct in the conflict between the Blues and the Greens. In 532 A.D., the Blues and the Greens joined forces in rebelling against Emperor Justinian the Great.

First erupting in the Hippodrome, the "the Nika riots," as they were to be called in history (Nika, meaning, "to conquer"), soon spread out to the entire city. The fire that broke out during the ensuing tumult resulted in the destruction of Hagia Sophia. The

Emperor, who had accepted defeat and was about to flee, managed to save his crown on account of his wife, the Empress Theodora, who had dispatched Generals Narces and Balisarius to suppress the rebellion. The Palace Guards, attacking the rebels, restored law and order by putting tens of thousands of them to the sword.

Unfortunately, despite the suppression of the rebellion on January 13, 532, flames consumed Hagia Sophia for the second time.

During the excavations carried out by A.M. Schneider in 1935 in the western courtyard of Hagia Sophia, many large marble slabs embellished with lambs in relief, representing the twelve apostles, were unearthed. It was subsequently discovered that these slabs were actually fragments of an entrance of monumental dimensions. Apparently, these are the remains of the front entrance of the second Hagia Sophia, which had been built by Emperor Theodosius II in the form of a basilica.

It was this second Hagia Sophia, the remains of which we see today, that was burned down during the Nika riots. We learn from Procopius, the Byzantine historian of the period, that as soon as the rioting mob was crushed, Emperor Justinian took steps to build an edifice that would be entirely different from its earlier models – one that would be the most majestic and gigantic temple ever built.

Icon of St. Eudoxia. The icon is inlaid with precious, colored stones, and dates from the Byzantine period. Istanbul Archaeological Museum.

A bust of Emperor Arcadius. 4th century. Istanbul Archaeological Museum.

The Construction of Hagia Sophia for the Third Time

Bloodily suppressing the Nika Insurrection, Emperor Justinian undertook the construction of a new church where Hagia Sophia, which had burned to the ground on January 13-14, 532, once stood. The Byzantine historian Procopius, who lived during the same period and wrote about the life and deeds of the Emperor, reported that the new project was taken up on February 23, a mere thirty-nine days after the fire.

Emperor Justinian assigned two architects, Isidorus, the Elder, a Milesian by birth, and Anthemius of Tralles, to built the new church. Anthemius had numerous brothers. One of them was Metrodorus, who was a grammarian of distinction; another one was Olympius, a famous jurist, and Diochorus and Alexandros, who were doctors of renown in their time. As for Isidorus, the Elder, he collected the writings of Archimedes, the famous mathematician of Antiquity; and we owe to Isidorus the preservation of these precious texts. Both Anthemius and Isidorus, the Elder, have left us a collection of texts on various technical subjects.

Justinian had materials for his new church brought from all over his empire. This included the columns of all the temples spread throughout Asia Minor. Among these were those of the Temple of Artemis at Ephesus. Justinian went so far as to have stones of various colors brought from far distant quarries in Egypt and Thessaly. According to various old sources, more than ten thousand workers were employed under one hundred foremen in the building of the church. This construction, carried out in accordance with a new plan, took five years. The completed church was opened on December 27, 537, accompanied by the sacrifice of one hundred oxen,

Two different views of Hagia Sophia. First built in 360, Hagia Sophia was burned to the ground in 404, only to be rebuilt and opened for worship again in 415. The building was razed once again by fire 532. Emperor Justinian had the church rebuilt in its present form, where upon it was reopened for worship in 537.

After Fatih the Conqueror took Istanbul and transformed Hagia Sophia into a mosque, a brick minaret was built in its southeast corner. The two minarets in front of Hagia Sophia were built by Mimar Sinan during the reign of Murad III (1574-1595).

six thousand sheep, six hundred stags, one thousand pigs, ten thousand hens and ten thousand roosters. Justinian came to this inauguration and consecration ceremony holding hands with the Patriarch. Upon seeing the grandeur of the church, he spoke these words, "My thanks and gratitude to my Lord for granting me the means for creating such a glorious place of worship!" It is known, however, that the building was not entirely complete at that time. For example, the mosaics embellishing the interior were not completed until the time of Emperor Justin II (565-578).

Although Hagia Sophia filled one with awe and admiration because of the originality of its

architecture, the greatness of its dome and the boldness of its creation and the magnificence of its inner decoration, it had not yet acquired static equilibrium. Repairs were undertaken because the great dome and the half-dome in the eastern part of the church had cracked due to earthquakes in August 553 and on December 14, 577. But on May 7, 558, the main dome collapsed completely. As a result of the debris piling up in the interior, the altar and the ciborium covering it, as well as the ambon (pulpit) were crushed. Emperor Justinian asked for immediate restoration, and entrusted Isidorus, the Younger, the nephew of Isidorus, the Elder, with the reconstruction work. This architect constructed the dome out of

Seen in front of Hagia Sophia are the tombs of the Ottoman Sultans. Built by Mimar Sinan, they belong to Selim II, Murad III (1546-95) and Mehmed III (1595-1603). The Baptistery was transformed into a tomb for Sultans Mustafa I and Ibrahim. The building seen in the very front is the Haseki Hürrem Sultan Hamam (Bath).

A golden reliquary cover that was plundered during the Latin Invasion. 10th century.

Incense burner in the shape of the Hagia Sophia. Plundered during the Latin Invasion in the 12th century.

lighter materials and elevated it about seven meters. The reopening took place on December 23, 562. On the occasion of these second inauguration ceremonies, a palace official named Paul, the Silentiary, who was also a contemporary Byzantine poet, wrote a long epic poem describing and praising the greatness, the beauty and the grandeur of Hagia Sophia. This eulogy, known as Ekphrasis, is an invaluable source for the architectural and decorative characteristics of the sixth-century Hagia Sophia.

Hagia Sophia was the scene of many events throughout the entire history of Byzantium. Emperors were crowned and victories celebrated there; and wrongdoers sought asylum in this sanctuary because of the immunity provided by the Church. Equally important, foreigners of various nationalities who came to Istanbul paid visits to this great church and architectural monument, leaving full of awe. It is reported that the people entering the service of the church at that time numbered six hundred. It is also known that all religious pictures and figures were removed from Hagia Sophia 726–842, a period known in history as "Iconoclasm." Pictures, e.g., icons, were supposedly akin to idolatry, hence the hostility towards them. The adherents of this movement were known as iconoclasts. They were literally "image breakers." One of the strong advocates of this movement was Emperor Theophilus (829-842), who, in order to prove that Hagia Sophia was worthy of his imperial attention, had two wings

A view of the magnificently decorated columns and dome. Along the edge of the dome are figures of angels, called Seraphim.

Colorful marble plating, brought from a variety of places, placed side-by-side to create decorative motifs. The columns inside were brought from such edifices of antiquity as the Heliopolis Sun Temple and the Ephesus Temple of Artemis.

of a bronze door of an ancient edifice installed at the southern entrance to the church. On the surface of these doors, which are still there today, one can see the monograms of the Emperor.

Hagia Sophia suffered a great fire in 859. But it received the greatest damage in the earthquake of January 8, 869, during which one of its half-domes in the west of the building collapsed. Emperor Basil I

The lower and upper galleries of the southern section of Hagia Sophia, and the columns that support them.

A general look at the interior of Hagia Sophia and one of the large Hellinistic earthenware urns brought from Pergamon.

(867-886) immediately ordered the necessary repairs to be made. During these years, Orso Partetsipatio, the Doge of Venice, presented the Byzantine emperor with the gift of a bell to be hung in Hagia Sophia.

An earthquake occurring on the eve of 25-26 October, 989 resulted in the destruction of the great dome and many parts of the building. Reigning at that time was Basil II (976-1025), who restored the church to its former status through a six-year-period of repairs carried out by an architect by the name of Tridat. The sacred building was re-opened for church services on May 13, 994. The long duration of the repairs indicate the severity and magnitude of the damage caused by the earthquake.

Since Hagia Sophia was the greatest religious center of Byzantium, a great many of the ceremonies held by the Emperor and the Patriarch took place there. Emperor Constantine VII Porphyrogenetos (913-919) provided all the details of these ceremonies in his Book of Ceremonies, which is an important source of information on the tenth century. Important religious gatherings were held in Hagia Sophie in the southern gallery on the upper floor. Decrees made at the assembly held in 1166 were hung on the wall. Only copies of them are available today.

The Fourth Crusade originally headed for Jerusalem but changed its course in 1203 and came to Istanbul instead. Emperor Alexius IV, who was in debt to the Latins, was forced to give them many precious objects from Hagia Sophia. When the Latins of the Crusading Army captured the city in 1204, they looted and ransacked it, confiscating whatever items of value they could find in Hagia Sophia as well as other churches. In addition to the general

plundering of churches that occurred during the first few days of confusion, Hagia Sophie was vandalized. The altar of the Virgin Mary was demolished, wine was drunk from chalices used in religious ceremonies, and pack animals were taken into the church, where they were loaded with the plundered objects. If one is to believe the thirteenth-century Byzantine historian Nicetas Acominatus, a prostitute mounted the pulpit, and sang and danced there. During this plundering, many holy relics such as "a portion of the True Cross," a stone from the tomb of Jesus, the Virgin Mary's milk, the shroud of Jesus, and bones of many saints preserved in valuable cases were all taken out of Hagia Sophia and sent to churches in the West. Today, all the relics sent in 1204 are on display in various museums in Europe.

After the cessation of the initial desecration, Hagia Sophia fell into the hands of the Venetians. Though there was constant bickering due to their refusal to share administration of Hagia Sophia with other Catholics, five emperors were crowned here during the Latin occupation, which continued up to 1261. The stone slab with the inscription Enrico Dandolo, seen on the floor of the upper story of Hagia Sophia, was rumored to the tomb of the Venetian Doge, who died there after having worked for a long time to seize Istanbul from the Byzantines. This rumor was challenged during the restorations conducted during the last century (1847-49), leading to the conclusion that this engraving had been done

The interior of Hagia Sophia. The domed basilica-type building consists of a large central nave, flanking naves on the northern and southern sides, and two nartexes on the western side. The 100-meter long building measures 79.30 meters from the Imperial Gate to the apse alone.

so as to create a symbolic burial site to keep alive the memory of Dandolo. When the Byzantines recaptured the city and revived the Empire in 1261, Hagia Sophia was in extremely dilapidated condition. The four supporting buttresses in the west were very likely built at that time. In 1317, Emperor Andronicus II (1282-1328) had supporting buttresses built in the eastern and northern parts of the building in order to strengthen them. The violent earthquake in October 1344 created new cracks in Hagia Sophia, which contributed to collapse of various parts of the building on May 19, 1346, two years later. The major earthquake led to the collapse of the eastern arch together with the eastern part of the dome, as well as damage in other sections. As the Byzantine Empire was in no financial state to meet the expenses needed for repairs, the church remained closed for some time. The repairs, however, were undertaken in 1354 by means of levying special taxes and collecting donations. It is known that the restoration was carried out by two Latin architects, Astras and Peralta.

The travelers visiting Istanbul at the beginning of the fifteenth century tell of ruins in the vicinity of Hagia Sophia and that the church itself was in a state of neglect and disrepair, with many of its doors having fallen off and strewn about on the ground. When the Turks conquered Istanbul in 1453, Hagia Sophia was in a devastated state.

There are 107 columns inside Hagia Sophia. The most important of these are in the lower part of the building. Some of them were brought by the Emperor from various locations, and ancient buildings and temples.

The southern nave of Hagia Sophia. The structure seen on the left side of this nave is the Library of Mahmud I. The ceiling of the nave is decorated with gilded mosaics from the 6th century.

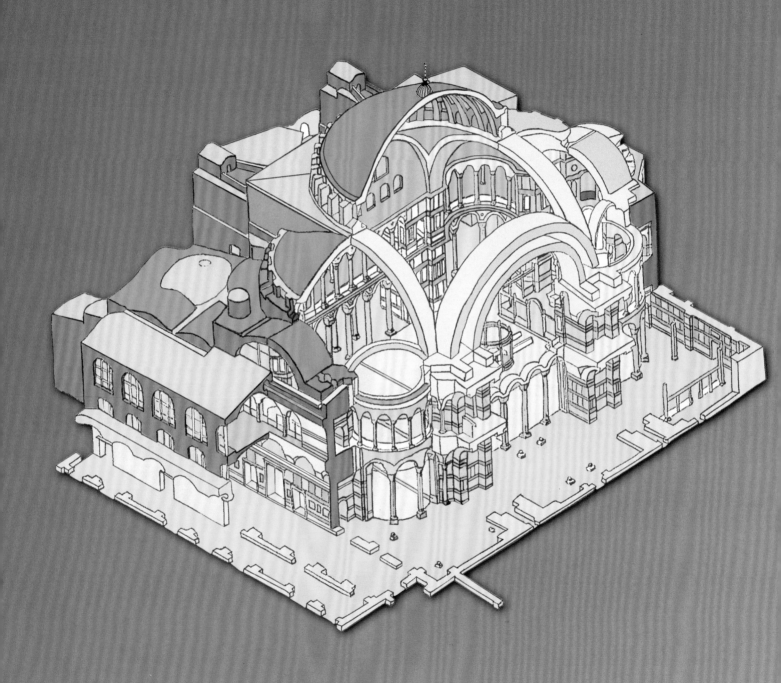

Touring Hagia Sophia

On November 24, 1934, it was decided to convert Hagia Sophia into a museum. The entrance to the mosque is made from the west. Just after going by the ticket booths, one enters a broad courtyard. During the time of Justinian, it had a columned porch and a fountain for ablutions in the middle, called the Phiale. The Byzantines would go inside after washing at this fountain. In old sources that have survived, it is noted that there was an inscription that read: "Do not only wash your hands and faces here, but your hearts as well." It is known from old pictures that these columns, which were linked to one another with arches, were still intact in the 1870s. The floor of the courtyard was a great deal lower than its present level.

It is claimed that during the Byzantine period, the Patriarchate was located where the fountain for ablutions and the school for boys, both of which were built by Sultan Mahmud I, are today.

The school for boys, facing the fountain for ablutions, is a single-domed simple building constructed by Sultan Mahmud I in 1739. Today this building is used as the library of the museum. The fountain for ablutions was also built by Mahmud I, but a year later, in 1740. It rests on eight slender columns supporting eight pointed arches. Decorative in style, the fountain is ornamented with a bronze network on which floral designs are engraved, and is encircled with an inscription of a panegyric poem commemorating the date. East of the fountain for ablutions and beside the route from which Hagia Sophia is exited there is a charitable public fountain.

The Baptistery, which is located in the southern part of Hagia Sophia, was converted in the Ottoman period into tombs for Sultans Mahmud I and Ibrahim. The old Skevephylekion, referred to as the Treasury

Front page: An aerial view of Hagia Sophia. One of the largest churches in the world, it has remained intact for almost 1500 years.

A cross-section of Hagia Sophia.

The first edifice that we come across when we walk through Hagia Sophia is the şadırvan. Built during the reign of Mahmud I and completed in 1740, it is held up by eight marble columns.

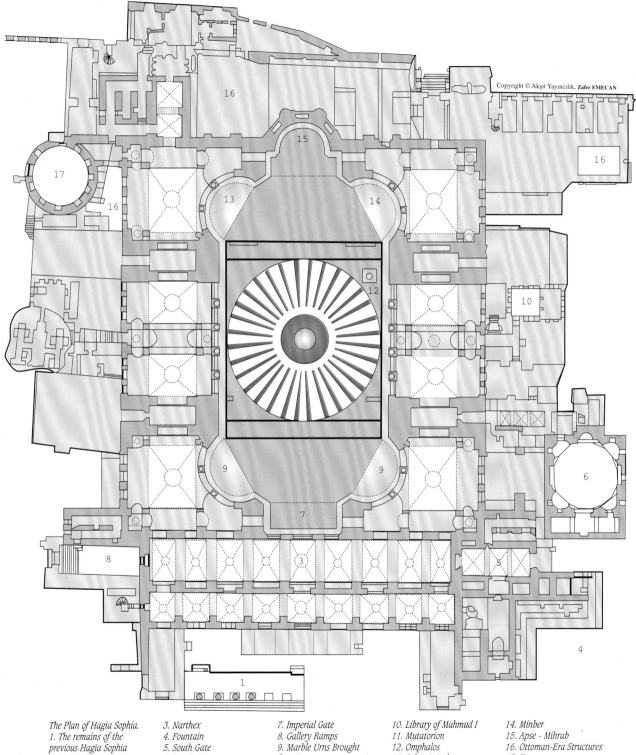

Copyright © Akşit Yayıncılık, **Zafer EMECAN**

The Plan of Hagia Sophia.
1. The remains of the previous Hagia Sophia
2. Exonarthex

3. Narthex
4. Fountain
5. South Gate
6. Baptistery

7. Imperial Gate
8. Gallery Ramps
9. Marble Urns Brought from Pergamon

10. Library of Mahmud I
11. Mutatorion
12. Omphalos
13. Sultan's Lodge

14. Minber
15. Apse - Mihrab
16. Ottoman-Era Structures
17. Treasury

35

Building, has a different entrance today and is being used as an office building. The old suite for trustees is used as the administrative headquarters of the museum, the adjacent muvakkithane, which was constructed by Sultan Abdulmecid, is used as offices for the museum, and the sebil (charitable public fountain) next to the fountain for ablutions is used as a warehouse for the tomb.

One can see many architectural remains in the courtyard of Hagia Sophia. They include those of the Fatih Medrese, situated in the east of the courtyard.

The remains near the entrance to Hagia Sophia are those belonging to the Hagia Sophia church built at the time of Emperor Theodosius. Located in a huge hole two meters in depth, are vestiges of the steps of a staircase and pieces of architectural edifices with reliefs of lambs, dating back to the old Hagia Sophia.

After the conclusion of our tour in the courtyard, let us now proceed to enter the interior of the outer narthex though the triple doors. This section, free of ornaments, has nine parts with vaults and is 5.75 m in width. It does not display any distinguishing architectural characteristics. Today, a small collection of Byzantine stonecutting and masonry work is exhibited here. These are panels of mosaics, works of stone, a baptismal font, slabs with reliefs and copies

The door of the southwest vestibule. Brought from a Hellenistic temple near Tarsus, it is beautifully decorated. It was put here in the 9th century by Emperor Michael. Afterwards, it was embellished with the monograms of various emperors.

The door of the southwest vestibule opening into the interior nartex. Above the door is a picture of the Virgin Mother with the Christ Child on her lap. In her left hand is Constantine I holding a model of the city, while in her right hand is Justinian embracing a model of Hagia Sophia.

of the Synode resolutions made in 1166, engraved on marble and collected by Emperor Comnenos. They are all from Hagia Sophia or its environs. Besides these, one can see the tughra (monogram) of Sultan Abdulmecid, made from the pieces of fallen mosaics collected during the restoration undertaken by Fossati in the years 1847-1849.

The Inner Narthex

Five different doors lead to the inner narthex, the width of which is 9.55 meters. The surfaces of the doors, which are made of oak wood, are plated with bronze. The narthex is divided up into nine parts with arches that are parallel to the axis; the walls are covered with marble. Compared to the outer narthex, the inner narthex is higher and richer in ornamentation. It is this ornamentation, which consists of mosaics of geometric figures against a gilded surface, has helped to maintain the original grandeur of Saint Sophia up to the present. The ceiling of the narthex is completely adorned with mosaics. The southern door, which is presently used as an exit from the museum, was formerly called the Horologion and was used exclusively by the emperors during religious ceremonies. The bronze wings of a door taken out of a temple in Tarsus and

A detail from the handiwork done on the door of the western vestibule.

A view of the ceiling adornments, the doors opening into the main chamber, and the interior nartex. The main building is entered from the interior nartex through nine doors. The three in the west were set aside for the public, while the three in the north for those seeking refuge; the ones in thee middle, were reserved for the emperors. On the bronze casting of the doors, there are interesting legendary scenes.

brought to Istanbul in 838 by Emperor Theophilus (829-842) were installed on this door. The gilded panels over these wings that belonged to the Hellenistic period were torn down and taken away during the invasion of the city in 1204 by the Latins.

There is a panel of mosaics in this section situated over the door leading to the inner narthex. On it is a depiction of Constantine I presenting the Virgin Mary with a model of Istanbul, as well as Justinian the Great, offering her one of Hagia Sophia. In the northern part of the inner narthex, there is a ramp leading to the upper gallery.

The main hall of Hagia Sophia is reached by going through nine doors in the inner narthex. The three doors in the middle were reserved for the emperors. Of these, the one in the middle is framed in

A detail of the decorations in Hagia Sophia. In addition to geometric motifs upon a gold-gilded background, circular motifs were also used.

bronze, with wings made of thick oak plated with bronze sheets. On these sheet plates are stylized figures in relief of plants and crosses coming out of bowls.

The door in the middle was for the exclusive use of the emperors. The emperors would enter the main body of the church after bowing down. The golden ornaments covering these doors were also taken away during the Latin invasion. On the mosaics located over the door for the emperors, Emperor Leon VI is portrayed bowing. After having examined these mosaics, let us now proceed to the main hall.

Most of the mosaics seen in various places, particularly in the interior nartex and upper gallery, consist of geometric designs, and are carry-overs from the first Hagia Sophia.

Back page: A mosaic tableau on the southwestern door of the nartex.

ΙΟΥΟΟΙΟ
CΤΙΝΙΛΝΟC
ΙΛΜΟCΒΑCΙΛΕ
ΛΘΟΙC.

ΜΡ

The Mosaics Over the Southwestern Entrance

On the door that leads to the narthex from the south, there is a triple panel of mosaics. This panel of mosaics, which has survived intact, was found during the restoration carried out by G. T. Fossati in 1849. Against a background of golden mosaics, Mary is portrayed in the middle, with Emperor Constantine I on her right, and on her left, Emperor Justinian the Great.

The Virgin is sitting on a throne without a back, holding the Christ Child on her lap. The Virgin's feet rest on a pedestal covered with silver mosaics, whose border is embellished with precious stones. The Virgin, as is always the custom in Byzantine art, is clad in dark blue attire. Flanking her head are medallions, on which there are monograms (MP-OY), which express the words Mater and Theou, meaning "the mother of God." The Christ Child, seen on his mother's lap, is making the sign of blessing while holding a scroll in his left hand. The expression on his face is that of an adult rather than of a child.

To the left of the Virgin, Emperor Constantine

Mosaics on the western entrance of the nartex. On these mosaics, which date from 944, Mary is holding the Christ Child on her lap; on her right, Constantine is presenting her with the city, while on her left, Justinian is handing her the church. On both sides of the head of Mary are disks, within which there are monograms.

Justinian in ceremonial attire handing a model of Hagia Sophia to Mary. Next to Justinian is the inscription, "The exalted sovereign Justinian."

(306-337) is presenting a model of the city to Mary. Beside the Emperor, there is an inscription in dark-blue letters on a background of golden mosaics, running from top to bottom, stating the following: "Great Emperor Constantine among the Saints." The founder of Christian Istanbul is portrayed here not in the garments of his period (e.g., the 4th century), but those of the period when the mosaics were made (e.g., the 10th century). The Emperor, who is wearing a dark-colored robe, and a shawl with gold

and silver embroidery on top, has a crown on his head.

To the right of the Virgin is Emperor Justinian the Great, (527-565). The Emperor is offering Virgin Mary a model of Hagia Sophia. The Virgin Mary was proclaimed to be the protector of the city after the siege of the city in 626 by the Avars, who had brought great despair to the Byzantine people. These mosaics were made as part of the restoration done 968–984, during the reign of Basil II.

Constantine is presenting a model of the city to Mary. The inscription behind the Emperor says, "Constantine, a great saint and sovereign." The Emperor is wearing ceremonial attire.

The Mosaics Above the Imperial Gate

The gate that is located in the western part of Hagia Sophia, on the same axis as the apse, is the Imperial Gate. As the name indicates, this gate was used by the emperors in the ceremonies they held. The semi-circular space above it is decorated with mosaics.

In the middle of the scene depicted, Jesus Christ is sitting on a throne above a floor made of gold. This throne, which is a replica of the Byzantine throne, is ornamented with pearls and precious stones. While sitting on this throne, Christ Pantocrator makes a sign of blessing with his right hand. He holds in his left hand an open book in which a quotation from the Bible of Hagia John reads as follows in Greek: "Let peace and safety be with you. I am the peace and glorious light of the universe." Jesus here, whose feet rest on a pedestal, has an expression and outlook similar to the statues of Aesklepios, the god of good health of antiquity. Hence, the quality of Christ as God and Savior is manifested through an expression taken from the art of Antiquity.

At either side of Christ's shoulders, there is a medallion. The one on the right contains a portrayal of Mary, Mother of Christ, while the one on the left has one of the Archangel Gabriel, the founder of the church.

An emperor is bowing down in front of the throne. This is Leon VI, who was in power between 886-912. Given these dates, we can conclude that these mosaics were made either at the end of the ninth, or at the beginning of the tenth centuries.

These mosaics, which could be seen until the middle of the 18th century, are the first ones to have been cleaned by Theodore Whittemore in 1932.

The Imperial Gate. There is a mosaic of Leon VI on the gate. In the center of this mosaic, which dates to the 920s, Jesus is sitting on a throne and Emperor Leon VI is bowing down in front of him. On the left-hand-side of the medallion that is on the mosaic is the Virgin Mother while on the right is the Archangel Michael. Jesus is making the sign of blessing with his right hand; on his left hand is an inscription that says, "Peace be upon you, I am the light of the world."

The Main Hall of Hagia Sophia

It is possible to enter the main hall (Naos/Nave) through nine different doors from the inner narthex. The center of worship in Hagia Sophia, it has a width of 32.27 meters and is separated from the side naves by means of four quadrangular supporting columns, with pillars and monoliths placed in between. Including the side naves, the area is 70.30 x 69.50 meters in breadth. The length, on the other hand, reaches 100 meters when the inner and outer narthexes are included. With a plan of this scale, Hagia Sophia ranks fourth in the world after Hagia Peter in Rome, and the Cathedrals of Sevilla and Milan.

The dome that covers the main body is supported by four enormous piers and is 55.60 meters high. Due to its numerous repairs, the dome has lost its roundness and has become elliptical; thus, the diameter of the dome varies between 31.24 and 30.86 meters. Formerly the dome had a broadly spread out shape, but after it toppled in 558, a new dome was constructed with forty framed ribs and forty windows. In order to reduce the weight of the dome, two large half-domes and two exedras were added on the east-west axis; the weight was decreased by means of a system of arches, columns and vaults. In spite of all these measures, the weight of the dome constituted a problem in the earthquakes that have taken place throughout the centuries. By building buttressed supporting from the outside,

Byzantine and Ottoman architects provided for the conservation of the edifice up to the present.

The sheathing of the large carrying pillars with colorful slabs of marble and such stones as jasper had the effect of camouflaging them, resulting in the nave

An interior view of Hagia Sophia. On either side of the picture can be seen the northern and southern galleries and a part of the apse.

The Imperial Gate opening into the main hall.

becoming more illuminated. Because of this, the dome grew to be more pronounced.

Old sources inform us that underneath the calligraphic inscription from the Holy Koran, (written by Kazasker Mustafa İzzet Efendi) at the center of the dome that we see today there used to be mosaics of Jesus. It is known that there was a cross there in the sixth century, and that the mosaics of Jesus were made after 842. These mosaics were damaged in 989, and had fallen off completely by 1346. They were replaced by mosaics of Christ Pantocrator (Ruler of the Universe) made on a medallion eleven meters in diameter in 1355, during the reign of Emperor John Paleologos. It is not known if the mosaics of Christ still exist under the calligraphy.

Upon examination of the easternmost of the four

Many modifications were made to the interior of Hagia Sophia during the Ottoman period. These include the minber and large inscription-containing panels seen in the photograph.

arches supporting the dome, it was discovered that there were mosaics of Jesus Christ, Virgin Mary, John the Baptist and Emperor John V Paleologos.

On the vault of the bema in Hagia Sophia, there are figures of two angels, which represent the Archangels Gabriel and Michael, dating back to the ninth century. Gabriel, on the right, is in fairly well preserved condition, but Michael, on the left, has almost completely deteriorated; only the tips of his wings have survived. These archangel figures are portrayed in ceremonial garbs of dark colors over a gilded surface.

On the pendentive enabling passage to the main dome, there are four distinct figures of angels. In

The colossal dome of Hagia Sophia. 55.60 meters high and 31.36 meters wide, this magnificent dome sits upon four great marble beams. A portion of the weight of the dome is taken up by the half-domes in the east and west. There are Seraphim in each of the four corners of the dome.

contrast to the eastern-situated ones, which are originals, the western-oriented ones were completed with frescoes after having deteriorated. While these figures were never concealed during the Ottomans, their faces were covered by stars during the restoration done by Fossati.

The semi-arched niches of the northern tympanon (windowed walls) of Hagia Sophia were decorated with golden mosaics of patriarchs. More will be said about them when the Virgin Mary mosaics found in the apse are discussed.

The light filtering in from the windows of the walls of the tympanon considerably illuminates the main body. The floor is covered with rectangular slabs of marble, which conceals the original pavement.

The main body of Hagia Sophia is partitioned from the side naves on the right and left by four large columns with colonnades running between them. The naves vary in width from between 18.20 and 18.70 meters. Of the monoliths and columns found in Hagia Sophia, forty are on the lower floor and sixty-seven are located on the upper-floor ("triforium") galleries. The columns, which were brought from temples located all over the empire, have capitals that are illustrative of Byzantine craft of stone ornamentation. On these capitals, which date back to the sixth century, are monograms of Emperor Justinian, the

A view of the magnificent lower and upper galleries. These galleries are held up by columns on whose capitals are the monograms of Justinian and his wife Theodora. The fine workmanship on these capitals is reflective of the most glorious period of Byzantine art.

Great, and his wife, Empress Theodora. The eight colossal columns of green porphyry on the lower floor were brought from the Temple of Artemis at Ephesus, while the dark purple ones were hauled from Thebes in Egypt. The walls are plated with marbles from Thessaly from the floor up to the level of the arches. Furthermore, the walls were made more attractive and pleasing to the eye through the use of Egyptian porphyry, marbles from Numidia and pink-veined marbles from Phyrigia.

The two alabaster urns located at the entrance belong to the Hellenistic Age and were brought from Pergamum. Located between two buttresses in the middle of the nave on the southern side is the library of Mahmud I. We shall deal with this library and the other items of the Turkish period in a separate chapter.

Under the eastern half-dome of the main body, the bema and apse sections are located. These parts were separated from the main body in Byzantine times by a railing. This was where the holy articles of the church and the relics of the Saints were kept. Moreover, on the step-like raised platforms, the patriarchs and dignitaries of the church used to sit. During the Ottoman period, the present-day mihrab

One of two marble earthenware urns inside Hagia Sophia. These water urns, which belong to the Hellenistic Era (e.g., the 3rd century B.C.), were brought during the time of Murad III from Pergamon and placed inside the mosque.

The western nave. The width of the central nave is 32.27 meters. Together with the northern and southern naves, this width reaches 70 meters.

Decorative marble embellishments on the interior side of the Imperial Gate. On the right and left, stylized dolphins and the winnowing fork of Poseidon are carved inside circular ornamentations. Between these two panels, there is a panel resembling an altar.

was constructed in the apse. The two candelabra flanking the mihrab were presented by Süleyman the Magnificent after his successful Hungarian campaign. The Turkish works here, the mihrab and the inscription on top of it, the panels, the minber, and the muezzin's loggia shall be dealt with in a separate chapter.

The area made up of round pieces of stone in front of the loggia of the muezzin was the place called the "Omphalion." This was where the coronation of emperors took place. In the naves on either side of it, there are pictures engraved on stone slabs that form special panels. Some of these panels are located behind the Imperial Gate. On the right and left,

stylized dolphins and the winnowing fork of Poseidon are carved within circular ornamentations. Between these two panels, there is a panel resembling an altar and behind the curtain between the columns there is a cross.

In the northern nave, there is a quadrangular column located near the exit doors. This column, sheathed with brass plates and has a hole in the middle, is known as the "the sweating column." By inserting a finger into this hole, one was supposed to make a wish. Let us make our wish and then proceed to the upper galleries.

One of the marble panels above the door. Marble brought from many different places in the Byzantine Empire was used in the interior design of the church.

The Upper Galleries

Walking over the ramp situated south of the inner narthex, we head to the upper galleries of Hagia Sophia. It used to be possible to reach the upper galleries from both sides, but today this ramp is the only way they can be accessed.

The first section of the upper floor is an area, extending from end to end, that is covered with a cradle vault. This place, which was reserved for women, was formerly called the Gynekoion. Considerably illuminated by the light filtering in from the windows on the west, it resembles the halls of the Byzantine imperial palaces.

The section that has the appearance of a loggia, which opens into the main area where three arches are supported by double columns of green breccia, is outlined with colorful stones, indicating that it once was a place reserved for the empress. At the front of all the upper floor galleries, there are marble railings, covered front and back with ornamentations. On them it is possible to see inscriptions of people who visited Hagia Sophia throughout the centuries. Among these inscriptions are those of Vikings who came to Istanbul during the Byzantine period.

Particularly interesting are the wooden beams, on which six-century designs are engraved, stretching between the arches. The vault of this gallery is covered with decorations, imitations of those of the narthex below, which were added during the repairs undertaken between 1847-1849.

The door facing this gallery leads to the rooms that at one time were used as quarters for priests. Today they function as a warehouse for the icon collection. As gatherings were held under the Patriarch in the adjacent gallery, it is thought that

A view of one of the upper galleries. There are three upper galleries – north, south and west – in Hagia Sophia. Of these, the most important is the western gallery, which can be seen in the picture.

A loggia in the upper gallery reserved for the Empress and her attendants.

A detail from the marble door that opens into the southern gallery. This door, which separates the western and southern galleries, is a replica of the bronze doors used in antiquity. The door was probably built later to partition the gallery so that it could be used as a consul hall. This door was referred to by the people as the door that divided paradise and hell.

these rooms were reserved for patriarchs and bishops. They must be the place of the big and small Sekrata referred to in ancient sources. Though in very poor condition, some designs have survived. Among these are portraits of the Patriarchs. There are also mosaics of the Virgin and Jesus Christ, which must have been made in the second half of the ninth century. These rooms are closed to visitors today.

Let us now proceed to the southern gallery. Located above the southern nave, it is divided into two sections by means of a door that is made of imitation bronze. It was once held that on one side of the door stood paradise, while on the other side, hell. A set of panels covers the surface of one side of the door, with five panels located on each wing. On them are small compositions of religious subjects. Over time, these compositions have become effaced, with only such symbols as

few fish and some fruit surviving.

Inside this gallery, in the interior of the buttress on the right side after the partition, there is a small chapel, in which some fragmentary mosaics are still visible. On the right wall of this gallery, which is well illuminated by the window on the side, there is a

A view of the center of the upper gallery. The capitals of the green-colored columns of the gallery are decorated with fine masonry while the arches between each column are embellished with mosaics.

prominent scene of Deesis. At the foot of the wall across from this scene stands a slab of stone with an inscription that is believed to mark the burial site of Enrico Dandolo, the Doge of Venice. At the end of the gallery turning to the bema, are the mosaics of Comnenos, which are some of the most magnificent mosaics in Hagia Sophia. After having carefully examined these mosaics as well as those of Zoë, let us now walk to the aisle between the exedra and the wall of the apse, to turn our attention to the Virgin Mary on the apse. A large piece of marble standing there has been transformed into a kind of lattice wall through artistic workmanship – giving it the effect of elegant lace.

If we immediately turn our backs upon entering the northern gallery, we can see the mosaics of Alexander. This gallery is very similar to the southern one in that only the above-mentioned mosaics exist there.

After having taken a look at the Deesis, Comnenos, Zoë, and Alexander mosaics in the upper galleries of Hagia Sophia, let us now conclude our tour of Hagia Sophia.

The Deesis mosaic on the southern part of the upper gallery. The panels in the middle of which is Jesus and on either side of him, Mary and John, are called the Deesis panels. On this panel, Mary and John the Baptist are asking Jesus to forgive mankind.

Another view of the center of the upper gallery.

The Mosaics in Hagia Sophia

Hagia Sophia was constructed between 532–537, upon the decree of Emperor Justinian (527-565), in the form that we see today. Over time, all of its surfaces, arches, vaults and domes, except its walls covered with marble pieces, were ornamented with mosaics, competing in beauty only with each other. Procopius, the historian-writer contemporary of Emperor Justinian, extols the incredible beauty of Hagia Sophia, the grandeur of its dimensions and the harmony of its scale. The fact that the interior decorations were made with the idea of creating only colorful and gilded surfaces has made it possible for them to survive until now. These decorations, which appear in the cross vaults of the inner narthex and on the interior of the vault on the right upon entering from the Imperial Gate consisted of golden mosaics at the time of Justinian the Great. It is not known with certainty whether the figural mosaics of that period survived or not. If they did, they must have been scraped away during the hostility of the Iconoclastic Period (726-842).

All the figurative mosaics that we see today in Hagia Sophia are those that were made after the conclusion of the Iconoclastic Period, e.g., starting in 867. The making of mosaics resumed once the Byzantine Empire reclaimed Byzantium in 1261. Since the mosaics were made at different points in time, however, they lack conformity in style and workmanship.

After the conquest of Istanbul by the Turks and the conversion of Hagia Sophia into a mosque, the mosaics in Hagia Sophia were not destroyed, but rather, after some time, covered with a thin coat of plaster. The mosaics remained in such a concealed state until the middle of the nineteenth century, when

A detail of the figure of Mary on the Deesis mosaic.

A cross mosaic. During the period of Iconoclasm ("hostility towards pictures": 726-842), figures of crosses were used instead of pictures as an element of decoration. After the end of this period, mosaics containing figures began to be used once again.

G. T. Fossati and his brother Guiseppe Fossati, who had come to build the Russian embassy, started to clean them in 1847, upon orders from Sultan Abdulmecid. This work continued until 1849. Once the plaster covering had been removed, the designs of the mosaics were sketched, with the intention of publishing them. This was not done, however. Instead, they were kept in an archive in Switzerland. The architect W. Salzenberg, who had been sent to Istanbul by the German Government during those years to help in the restoration of Hagia Sophia, extracted reliefs and sketched the designs once more, publishing them in 1854. After the conclusion of the work by the Fossati brothers, Sultan Abdulmecid visited Hagia Sophia and saw the mosaics. Eventually, he had them covered again, in an easily removable manner, in order to prevent their deterioration by the damp air.

In 1932, early in the period of the young Turkish Republic, the mosaics were cleaned once again – this time scientifically. Thomas Whittemore, working on behalf of the Byzantine Institute of America, had uncovered all of the mosaics by 1958 and subsequently published detailed sketches of them. Commenting on his work, Whittemore expressively stated, "Earthquakes and time have deprived the building of many mosaic masterpieces, but those

Column capitals with monogram. Each, superbly representative of 6th-century masonry, is an artistic experience in and of itself. They have the monograms of Emperor Justinian and his wife Theodora. The workmanship on the arches connecting them is of the same technique and refinement. As can be seen from the photograph on the left, wooden beams have been used between some of the columns. Only a few of them have survived till today.

remaining have been always well preserved by the Turks over the nearly five hundred years that they have used the building."

Aside from the mosaics we see in Hagia Sophia today, we know from various sources that there once were other mosaics that have not survived. We would like to briefly mention these mosaics, whose locations are not known, or which have been destroyed by the numerous earthquakes that have occurred over the ages – especially the one in 1894.

In the sixth century, there was a huge cross in the middle of the main dome in the interior of Hagia Sophia. This was replaced in 842 by a portrait of Jesus. These mosaics were also damaged in 889, after which mosaics of Christ Pantocrator were made instead - on a medallion eleven meters in diameter. These mosaics survived until the end of the seventeenth century. A beautiful calligraphic inscription later replaced them. This inscription, which contains Koranic Verses, was the work of Kazasker Mustafa Izzet Effendi. It is not known, however, whether or not the mosaics of Christ are still underneath.

Of the great arches carrying the main dome of Hagia Sophia, the one in the east was decorated with mosaics that depict the throne prepared for Jesus Christ. On the northern side of the arch, there were mosaics of Virgin Mary and right across from them,

A detail of the figure of Jesus on the Zoë mosaic making the sign of blessing with his right hand. This mosaic is one of the most beautiful examples of Byzantine mosaic art.

The Virgin Mary seen with the Christ Child in her lap in the Comnenos mosaic.

those of John the Baptist. On the lower tips of the arch, there was a portrait of Emperor John V Palailogos (1341-1391). At the beginning of the arch, there were figures of two eagles. It is now known that these decorations were made following the repairs in 1355.

In the middle of the western arch, there were portraits of the Virgin, and the apostles Peter and Paul on a medallion. This arch was badly damaged in the earthquake of 1894. Of the vaults located in the

Jesus holding the Bible in the Zoë Mosaic. He is holding a pearl-decorated Bible on his knees.

middle of the southern gallery, on the one in the east, there stood a great Pantocrator, and on the one in the west, there was a group of apostles.

In the chapels within the southern buttress, there are remains of badly damaged mosaics. While it is known that mosaics existed in the vaults of the northern gallery, they have not survived to the present. On the lower floor, on the door that Fossati called "the door for the poor," it is known that there were mosaics portraying a group of 5-6 persons.

A detail from above the door of the western vestibule. In the picture, Emperor Justininan is presenting Mary with a model of Hagia Sophia, which he has built.

Emperor Alexander Mosaics

The Emperor Alexander mosaics, situated at the southwestern end of the middle hall of the northern gallery, are some of the best-preserved mosaics of Hagia Sophia. No reason can be given as to why these mosaics were put in a place where they can hardly be seen. Born in 870, Alexander was the third son of Emperor Basil. Emperor Alexander is viewed on the panel from the front in a standing position. There are four medallions, two flanking each side, in which the name Alexander is written in full; and on the right, at the top, are his titles in monograms. The Emperor is clad in ceremonial robes embellished with pearls and precious stones, and is holding a bag in his right hand while holding a globe in his left hand. Emperor Leon VI (886-912), who is portrayed above the Imperial Gate in a position of prostration, is the brother of Alexander. It was Leon who insisted that Alexander share the throne with him. Alexander is recorded in history as having been an insignificant figure. During the years of partnership, Alexander left the affairs of state to his brother Leon, and indulged in debauchery, spending his time on pleasures and amusements. He was, in the end, forced to assume the reins of power alone in 912, after the death of his brother. But it was only thirteen months later that he passed away, too, at the young age of forty-three. These mosaics must have been made during the years between 912-913, when he reigned alone.

The Alexander Mosaic. Alexander, who shared power with his brother Leon, is depicted standing up. Because the figure is situated in an out-of-the way spot in the right corner of the northern gallery, it cannot be seen very well.

The Deisis Mosaics

On the upper floor of Hagia Sophia, the walls of the southern gallery are embellished with mosaics that are considered to be some of the best in Hagia Sophia and the most famous ones in the world. These are known as the Deisis Mosaics.

On these mosaics, Virgin Mary and John the Baptist (Ionnes Prodromos) are asking Jesus for intercession for humanity on the Last Judgment Day. The bottom parts of the 6 x 4.68-meter panel have unfortunately deteriorated due to the air current from the window. But even the remaining parts are sufficient enough to be considered the most important works of Byzantine art. The panel contains a large picture of Jesus in the middle, with the Virgin Mother on his right, and John the Baptist on his left, all of whom seen against a golden background. Jesus, who is here depicted from the front, has a halo, and a cross behind his head. While making a sign of blessing with his right hand, Jesus holds a bound Holy Book in his left hand. The bottom parts of the Virgin Mary, who is to the right side of Jesus, are badly deteriorated. Mary is shown in three-quarters profile; only her head and shoulders have survived the wear and tear of the years. She has a humane expression on her face and is looking downward. Both the names of Mary and Christ are abbreviated in Greek on both sides of their heads, respectively.

The figures of Jesus and John the Baptist on the Deisis Mosaic.

John the Baptist (Ionnes Prodromos) stands on the left side of Jesus. He is shown in three-quarters profile, just like the Virgin. While his first name is written in abbreviated form from top to bottom, Prodromos is written out in full. According to the Bible, John the Baptist spent his life in the desert, far away from the pleasures of the world, and this isolated, solitary life is reflected on the expression of his face. The suffering of human beings on the Last Judgment Day can be read on the faces of both the Virgin Mother and John the Baptist. They symbolize that salvation is through Christ on that fateful day. Christ, on the other hand, appears on this great judgment day as an entity full of tenderness and kindness, and exalted to reach divinity.

The well-chosen colors of the mosaics exemplify the extent to which the main principles of the pictorial arts of the Early Ages continued to live in both Byzantine art and the entire Middle Ages. The Deesis mosaics, which were uncovered through the meticulous work of Thunderwood from 1934 to 1935, are considered by the experts of art history as the beginning of the Renaissance in Byzantine pictorial arts. Although there is some disagreement among historians as to the origins of the Deesis mosaics, with some dating it to as far back as the 9th century, it is generally thought that they come down to us from the 12th century.

The bottom parts of the 12th century Deesis Mosaic have deteriorated over time. In the middle of the mosaic, Jesus is depicted, while on the left and right, respectively, are depictions of Mary and John the Baptist. The facial expressions of all three figures are immaculate. The face of Jesus, who is holding the Bible in one hand and making a sign of blessing with the other, is filled with compassion. The expression of the others, on the other hand, is clearly that of beseeching.

The Mosaics of the Comnenos

The mosaics of the Comnenos are located on the eastern wall of the southern gallery on the upper floor. On this panel, the Virgin Mary is depicted in the middle, flanked by Emperor John II Comnenos (1118-1143) and his wife Irene, who was of Hungarian origin. The Virgin Mary is holding the Christ Child on her lap. Behind the head of the Christ Child, there is a halo with a cross. Jesus is making a sign of blessing with one hand, while holding a scroll in the other. The Virgin is shown in her usual dark blue gown, standing up. On both sides of her head appear the signs "MP" and "OY," indicating her to be the Mother of God.

Emperor John II Comnenos is on the right side of the Virgin. Over the Emperor's head, the following words are written with red mosaics against a golden background; "Porphyrogennatos Ionnes Komnenos." The title of "Porphyrogennatos" is a sign of nobility used for those born during the reign of his father. John II Comnenos, who was one of the best emperors in Byzantine history, is depicted as a dignified person on these mosaics.

The Emperor, pictured from the front, is in a garb embellished with precious stones. He is holding a purse in his hand, which indicates that he has donated some money to Hagia Sophia.

To the left of the Virgin is Empress Irene, who is standing up, wearing ceremonial garments and has a crown on her head. Empress Irene was the daughter of King Laszlo of Hungary. With her elaborately

Emperor John II Comnenos and his wife Irene on the Comnenos Mosaic.

The Comnenos Mosaic is located in the eastern end of the southern gallery in Hagia Sophia. In the middle of the panel, which dates back to 1118, Mother Mary holding the Christ Child. To her left is Emperor John II Comnenos while to her right is his wife, Empress Irene.

plaited blond hair, light gray eyes and pink cheeks, it is clearly evident that she is from Central Europe. She is holding a scroll in her hand. On both sides of her head there is the inscription: "Pious Augusta Irene."

Near this triplex composition, a portrait of their eldest son Alexius Comnenos is squeezed in over an adjacent pilaster. It is known that this prince, who was made a partner to the throne in 1122 when he

was only seventeen, died soon thereafter of tuberculosis. Here, his face has mournful features, reflecting his sorry condition.

The mosaics of Comnenos were made in 1122.

They are some of the best examples of the display of realistic expression in the art of portraiture. Here, people are represented as they actually are, without being idealized.

The king on the mosaic is holding a sack, which symbolizes his having made a donation to Hagia Sophia. The Empress Irene, who is the daughter of the Hungarian king, is holding a scroll.

The Mosaics of the Virgin in the Half Dome of the Apse

The Virgin Mary mosaics are in the interior of the half-dome of the apse and are made against a golden background. These mosaics constitute some of the best mosaics in Hagia Sophia. As they are located in a very high location, they can hardly be seen from below. In order to see them clearly, it is necessary to walk up to the upper floor and view them up close.

Mary is portrayed sitting on a throne, with no back, that is studded with precious stones. The Virgin is wearing a dark blue garment and holding the Christ Child on her lap. Her feet rest on a pedestal embellished with precious stones. Mary's face was very successfully portrayed as regards to both its lines and the diffusion of colors on it

On the great arch of the apse, there used to be an inscription saying: "The pictures that were spoiled some time ago by imposters, were restored by capable and pious emperors." Today only the first three, and the last nine letters of this inscription are visible. Here, by referring to "imposters," the image-breaking Iconoclasts must be implied. As understood from this inscription, and from the speech delivered by Patriarch Photius on March 29, 867, the Virgin Mary mosaics were partially destroyed during the Iconoclasm movement, and were made once again right after its termination. These mosaics are the oldest in Hagia Sophia.

When examined carefully, defacement is discernible between the head and shoulders in the Virgin Mary mosaics. These disfigurements are the traces of a cross made after badly damaging the Virgin Mary mosaics. When this movement ended, the Virgin Mary mosaics were restored.

Although the Virgin Mary mosaics belong to the ninth century, the golden mosaics in the background date back to the sixth century.

The Virgin Mary Mosaic in the Apse. The mosaic comes down to us unharmed from the 9th century. In it, the Virgin Mother is holding Jesus in her lap. Mary is wrapped in a green mantle and is seated on a throne decorated with precious stones. The Christ Child, with a face full of maturity, is dressed in a gold-gilded cloak.

The Portraits of Angels on the Arch of the Bema

On the two sides of the large cradled vault in front of the apse, there are two portraits of angels facing each other. On the right, the Archangel Gabriel is depicted with wings. In contrast to the Archangel portrait on the right, which is fairly well preserved, the one on the left is very fragmentary, with only the tip of a wing of Archangel Michael surviving. These angel figures have also been done against a golden background.

The figure of Gabriel is standing with the tips of his wings hanging down. Gabriel is clad in a ceremonial robe typical of those worn by the notables of the Byzantine court. His inner garments, the skirts of which are embroidered in silver, are of a dark color. The loose cap he wears is ornamented with a wide band of golden embroidery. This is an attire of emperors or palace officials. He is holding a globe in his left hand and a scepter in his right land.

A great deal of painstaking care has been shown to portray the beautiful face of the archangel, whose hair is tied with a piece of ribbon. It is estimated that these archangel mosaics were made just after the Virgin Mary mosaics in the half-dome of the apse, e.g., towards the end of the ninth century.

A depiction of an angel on a bema arch. The winged Archangel Gabriel appears on this 9th-century mosaic. His left shoulder has been damaged.

The Mosaics of Empress Zoe

The mosaics of Zoë are situated on the eastern wall of the hall in the southern gallery reserved for emperors. This panel of mosaics, which is 2.40 x 2.44 meters in dimension, unfortunately lacks an approximately 35-centimeter portion at the bottom. On these mosaics, the figure of Christ Pantocrator is flanked by those of Emperor Constantine IX Manomachos and his Empress Zoë.

Christ is seated in the middle on a throne ornamented with precious stones. He is holding his right hand in a gesture of blessing, while holding with his left hand the Holy Book, studded with pearls, over his knees. Jesus is wearing a dark blue robe. The parts showing his feet are missing. There is a halo and a cross behind his head, on either side of which are the abbreviated monograms of "Iessus Christos," denoted with the letters "IC" and "XC."

On the right side of Jesus, Emperor Constantine IX Monomachos is depicted standing up, with his crown on top of his head, clad in ornate ceremonial costumes. He is holding a purse in his hand, symbolizing the donation he has made to the church. Over his head and against a golden background is an inscription to this effect: "Constantine Monomachos, the pious ruler of Romans and the servant of God's Jesus."

Standing to the left of Jesus is Empress Zoë – famed in Byzantine history for her many intrigues and marriages. The bottom parts of the Zoë mosaics are extremely deteriorated. The Empress is holding a scroll of papers, signifying the donations she has made. The inscription over the head of her third husband Constantine IX Monomachos (1042-1055) is repeated on this scroll. The Empress was the daughter of Constantine VII. Over the head of the Empress, there is an inscription to the effect: "Very pious Augusta Zoë." Although Empress Zoë appears

Constantine Monomuhos II as he appears to the left of Jesus on the Zoë Mosaic. The body of the Emperor, who, on this mosaic dating from 1042 is holding a moneybag, and is one of the last husbands of Zoë, was made for one of her former husbands. It is obvious that the head part of the figure was changed with each of her marriages. Above it is the inscription, "Sovereign of the Romans, Constantine Manomachos."

young in the mosaics, it is known that she was quite old even when she first got married in 1028 since the historians of her period state that she looked young because she was small and short. When examined carefully, the name of Constantine IX Monomachos can be seen to have been scraped away in two places; what remains today is unclear. The heads of previous emperors have been scraped off and replaced by the portrait we see there today. It is apparent from the mosaics on the neck of Zoë that her head was also altered at some point. These mosaics mostly likely represented other people in the past and were changed later on. It is suggested that either her first husband Romanos III Argyrus (1028-1034), or Michael IV, whom she adopted as a son first and made an emperor later on, were portrayed here. This Emperor, however, fell into disregard and was exiled to the Island of Prinkopo (of the Princess Islands). Subsequently, Zoë married Constantine IX, which was her third marriage. It is believed that in these mosaics, the head of this figure was scraped off and replaced by the head of Monomachos. But the fact that the head of Zoë was changed raises some questions. It may be a good guess that these mosaics were made for some other emperor and empress, and were used at the time of Zoë, by making changes to the parts where the heads were located. Belonging to the eleventh century, these mosaics provide us with a great deal of information about Byzantine palace dresses and the art of realistic portraiture.

The figure of Jesus on the Zoë Mosaic.

The Empress Zoë. Above the head of Zoë, who is holding a scroll, is the expression, "Zoë, the very pious Augusta."

The Mosaics Decorating the Walls of the Northern Tympanon

The semi-arched niches of the northern tympanon of Hagia Sophia are decorated with golden mosaics. Pictures of the Old Testament prophets were located at the beginning of a series of windows. On the lowest parts of the walls, the pictures of the patriarchs were located in procession in each of the seven niches. Only three of these pictures have been uncovered on the northern wall. These figures, which have been portrayed from the front, are placed in a frame having a rounded arch. Made against a golden background in the form of portraits, they were given the name, "Church Fathers."

In these figures, which appear according to a certain sequence, only the faces carry the characteristics of portraiture, while the bodies are practically identical. The figures depicted from the front and standing, have inscriptions in Greek next to each of them identifying who they are. Inside the first niche from the left is the figure of the young Hagia

The northern wall. This wall is held up by columns above and below it. Inside the niches on the northern wall are 10th-century portraits of religious men made from mosaics. The names of these saints, who are depicted in white ceremonial attire, are written next to them. Starting from the west, St. Ignatious (the Patriarch of Istanbul) occupies the first niche, St. Chrysostomos, the middle niche, and St. Ignatios Theophonus, the fifth niche.

The St. Chrysostomos Mosaic above the northern nave.

Ignatius, the Patriarch of Istanbul; in the fourth niche, the figure of Hagia John Chrysostomos, another Patriarch of Istanbul, and in the sixth niche, that of Saint Ignatius Theophorus, the Patriarch of Antioch. Very little has remained of the figure of Athanasius in the seventh niche. Here, all of the saints represented are clad in long robes, with crosses on their collars and on their skirts – attire peculiar to religious dignitaries. Their right hands are open at the level of their chests. With their left hands, evident under their mantles, they are holding the Holy Book ornamented with pearls. These mosaics were formerly in the form of a series of rows. On both walls, at the top and extending between the two series of windows, there was a long inscription, of which only a few letters are visible now. This inscription was in an ornate style and was to this effect: "This building, the apple in the eyes of the world, once again came under the protection of the Good Lord after being subject to much deplorable misfortune through time that threatened to destroy it; but this was averted with our help." As can be understood from this inscription, the decoration of mosaics on the tympanon walls is the achievement of an emperor who undertook to restore Hagia Sophia on a grand scale. Although it is not definitely known who this emperor was, it may, however, be surmised that they were made during the reign of Basil I (876-886). In other words, these mosaics can be dated back to the ninth century.

A view of the northern wall and the main dome.
One of the panels of saints on the northern wall.

Haiga Sophia During the Turkish Era

The siege of Istanbul began on April 6, 1453 and continued for fifty-three days before the city finally fell on Tuesday, May 29, 1453. When conquering Byzantium, the besieging Ottomans found both the city and the church in wretched condition. Many references are made to the sorry state of the city and Hagia Sophia in the various documents pertaining to the period. The many travelers who visited Istanbul then, among them in particular Pero Tafur, a Spanish nobleman from Cordoba, and Buondelmonti, the Florantine Traveler, point out the grim state of Hagia Sophia.

On Tuesday, May 29, 1453, Sultan Mehmed II, known as "the Conqueror," entered the city, riding at the head of his victorious army. Passing through the streets and along the Mese (the main street), he reached Hagia Sophia. After dismounting, he toured the galleries on the lower and the upper floors of Hagia Sophia. It distressed him very much to see such a sublime and magnificent place of worship in such pathetic condition. According to the accounts of Tursun Bey, the Ottoman historian who was present at the scene, the Sultan recited his famous couplet in Persian, expressing his grief at this sorry sight. From the records, we learn that he addressed the people, as well as the Patriarch and the church officials who had laid down in prostration. He said to the Patriarch: "Stand up. Look, I am Sultan Mehmed, telling you, your friends, and all those gathering here that as of today you have no reason to fear my wrath as regards to your lives and freedom." Then, turning around to his state officials and commanding officers, he ordered them not to mistreat the people, but rather to send them away to their homes in peace and safety.

The old framed inscriptions added to the building after it was transformed into a mosque during the Turkish era were replaced between 1847-49, during the reign of Sultan Addülmecid, by large disks 7.5 meters in diameter containing inscriptions done by the great calligrapher of the age, Mustafa Izzet Efendi.

A portrait of Fatih the Conqueror done by Bellini.

Mehmed the Conqueror then gave orders for the immediate cleaning up of Hagia Sophia. Upon seeing one of his soldiers defacing a piece of marble in the courtyard, he became furious. Running up to the soldier, he pushed him with his scepter, thus preventing further damage to the stone. He scolded the soldier by addressing him thus: "You are a good-for-nothing! How dare you try to harm a place of worship! If you are brave and man enough, try to build one yourself." Hammer Dueas narrates this incident as follows: "The soldier became half dead, not because of the shove by the scepter, but rather

because of the wrath of the Sultan; other soldiers carried him away from the courtyard. Thus, it was the thrust of this scepter that kept Istanbul intact, preventing the fall of even a single stone in the city during the tumult – the almost doomsday-like agitation and heedless confusion that surrounded the conquered city."

Even though he allocated a great deal of property for the maintenance of Hagia Sophia, Sultan Mehmed the Conqueror did not have many changes made to its interior. While it is thought that the minaret facing Sultanahmet Square was built during his era, it was

The iron latticework of the Şadırvan and the interior of the dome in the garden of Hagia Sophia. The iron latticework of the Şadırvan and its Baroque motifs are masterpieces of Ottoman ironworking.

Next Page: A general view of the Sultan Ahmed Mosque of Hagia Sophia.

later modified. The Fatih Medrese (Muslim school of theology), which is situated in the western part of Hagia Sophia, and of which only the foundations are visible today, was also constructed under Mehmed II.

It is known that a minaret was built during the reign of Beyazid II (1481-1512), who succeeded his father to the throne. This minaret must have been constructed as a replacement for the minaret built at the time of Mehmed the Conqueror. Beyazid II also had an additional floor to the Fatih Medrese made. Selim I, who ruled between 1512-1520, defeated the Mamluk Sultanate in Egypt in 1517, and brought the last Abbasid Caliph with him to Istanbul. This last Caliph, Al-Mutavakkul, proclaimed to the world that he transferred the caliphate to Selim I.

Süleyman the Magnificent, known to Turks as the "Süleyman the Law Giver," who succeeded his father Selim I and was in power between 1520-1566, made no changes to the mosque. But he did make a gift of two colossal candles on inverted bronze columnar bases that he had brought back all the way from Hungary, after the conquest of that country. These huge candelabra were placed on both sides of the mihrab.

Among the Ottoman sultans who showed interest in Hagia Sophia, first and foremost was Selim II, Süleyman's son, who ruled between 1566 and 1574.

The marble minber. One of the most beautiful examples of Turkish marble craftsmanship, the minber was added by Murad III. Its two flanking panels have been worked so as to have the appearance of lace. The same technique has been used above its entrance.

The main dome of Hagia Sophia and the engraved calligraphy inside it. This calligraphy was done by Mustafa Izzet Efendi with gold gilding. It is suspected that the figure of Pantacrator is under this inscription.

It is known that Selim II appointed Sinan, the most famous Turkish architect of all times, to conduct a restoration of Hagia Sophia. During that time, two minarets made of grooved brick were built. Sinan also undertook a long period of serious maintenance and restoration, which continued up to 1574, when Murad III succeeded Selim II to the Ottoman throne. Sinan demolished the houses surrounding the mosque and added two more minarets to Hagia Sophia. Sinan also constructed buttresses to support the walls of Hagia Sophia, which has enabled its survival up to the present. After the death of Selim II, his türbe (tomb) was located in the southern part of the mosque, so as not to detract from its grandeur. Several other tombs were subsequently built for Murad III and Mustafa I at Hagia Sophia. Later, in the interior of Hagia Sophia, a Hünkâr Mahfili (a sultan's gallery) covered with tiles, a minber (dais or a high pedestal with a staircase, on which a hutbe is delivered/pulpit) decorated with marbles, and a dais for a vaiz (sermon) and a loggia for a müezzin (a mosque official who calls Muslims to prayer, from the balcony of the minaret, five times a day) were built. During the reign of Murad III, two large alabaster urns

The Gallery of the Sovereign. In 1850, Abdülmecid had the architect Fossati build over the old gallery that had been used until the period of Mahmud II (1808-1830). The entrance is from the same door that is next to the Fountain of Ahmed III. The gallery replicates Byzantine art while at the same time conforms to the architecture of Hagia Sophia.

Also found are the inscription panels of Kazasker İzzet Efendi upon which Ottoman Sultans have written their names, and presented as gifts. These have been hung on the apse side of the picture. The two topmost inscriptions belong to Mahmud II, the lower left one, to Ahmed III, while the one without a signature in the lower right is thought to belong to Mustafa II.

were brought from Bergama (Pergamum) and placed on the two sides of the nave, as may still be seen today. Later on, two urns of the same type, with ornaments on their surface, were taken to Paris, where they are today on display at the Louvre Museum.

A devastating fire, which raged out of control for thirty-six hours, broke out in 1755. Beginning at the shore and extending up to Hagia Sophia, it caused the lead sheets covering the dome of Hagia Sophia to melt. In 1717, during the reign of Sultan Ahmed III, the plastering of Hagia Sophia was renewed. Outside the mosque, a beautiful flad›rvan (fountain for ablutions), a dining hall, an imaret (an almhouse, a kitchen for the distribution of food to the poor), and a sübyan mektebi (a school for boys) were built, while a new gallery for sultans and a new mihrab were put up inside the mosque. A magnificent library was also added. Moreover, the old Skvephylakion, which was referred to as the treasury building, was later converted into a warehouse for provisions.

During the reign of Sultan Mahmud II (1808-1839), eight hundred kese ("purse;" formerly

The tile panels dating from 1643 which are inside the apse have a depiction of Kabe on them. Not very many of them were made and are hence unique. This explains why there are so few of them and why they are so valuable.

The mihrap of Hagia Sophia. The former mihrap was renovated during the restorations carried out by Fossati in the 1850s. The candleholders in front of it were brought from Hungary during its conquest in 1526. Seen in the upper part of the mihrap, which is inside the apse - extending across it from top to bottom, is a strip of tiles upon which there is an inscription of a verse from the Koran. The verse on this strip of tiles, which dates from 1607, was written by a calligrapher by the name of Mehmed.

equivalent to five hundred piastres) were spent on repairs. Later, under Abdulmecid (1839-1861), much more extensive restoration was undertaken. The Swiss architect, Gaspare T. Fossati, who had come to Istanbul to construct the Russian embassy building, was assigned by Abdulmecid to handle the restoration of Hagia Sophia. G. T. Fossati, taking his brother Guiseppe Fossati with him, completed this assignment with the utmost care. The sum of forty thousand kese bequeathed to the State by the Sheik-

A tile panel dating from 1643 that is inside a vestibule.

A tile panel in the Mahmud I. Library.

ul-Islam (formerly the Minister responsible for all matters connected with the Sharia or Canon Law, religious schools, etc., who was second only to the Grand Vizier) Makkizadah Asim Effendi, was allocated to this restoration. This work, which was carried out by eight hundred workers, involved repairing the cracks and dangerous places, as well as the overhauling of all of the ornaments in the interior and the exterior of the mosque. While this work was being done, Fossati showed the mosaics to the

Sultan, who immediately gave orders that they be cleaned. The surfaces of the mosaics were carefully cleaned and covered again with a thin coat of plaster or paint that could easily be removed. The Sultan's tughra (monogram) was carefully made out of the mosaics that had fallen as a commemorative act.

The old-fashioned round-shaped chandeliers that had been installed during the time of Ahmed III were replaced by new pendulant ones. The square-framed inscriptions that had been suspended from columns

were removed, with circular-framed disks of gigantic proportion, hung there instead; these were inscribed by the calligrapher Kazasker İzzed Effendi (1801-1877) with the names of Allah, the Prophet Mehmed, Abu Bakr, Osman, Omar and Ali, the first four caliphs; and Hassan and Hüssain, the grandchildren of the Prophet.

Fossati painted the exterior of the mosque with yellow and red paint. He also removed the then-existing sultan's gallery, and built the present day

The Selim II Tomb made in 1577 by Mimar Sinan in the garden of Hagia Sophia. The octagonal tomb is decorated with 16th-century Iznik tiles and surrounded with a strip of tile containing scriptures from the Koran.

one to the left of the mihrab. This gallery is connected to the royal pavilion, built by Sultan Mahmud I, which is located behind the mosque. Moreover, a muvakkithane (a building made in order to keep time precisely for prayers) with a dome was built in the interior of the gate known as fiekerci kap›s› (Sugar Seller's Gate). Fossati also raised one of the minarets to the level of the others. The medrese, which was constructed at the time of Mehmed II and restored during the reign of Beyazid II, was rebuilt in a Western style. Only the foundations of this building can be seen today.

During these restorations, many celebrities, such as the Hungarian composer Franz Liszt, and Horace Vernet, the painter, visited Hagia Sophia. The architect W. Salzenberg, who came to Istanbul in those years, made sketches of the mosaics and published them after his return, without the permission of Fossati Brothers. Fossati himself was content with publishing an album showing only the interior and the exterior views of Hagia Sophia.

At the conclusion of all this restoration, the inauguration and re-consecration of Hagia Sophia took place on July 13, 1849 with ceremonial pomp.

The embellishments, created using the relief technique, inside the dome of the Tomb of Selim II, which was built by Minar Sinan, can be found in other tombs. For example, the Tomb of Murad III, built by Architect Davud Ağa, and the Tomb of Mehmed III, built by Sedefkar Mehmed Ağa in 1608.

The tile-embellished entrance door of the Tomb of Selim II. There are tile panels on either side of the entrance door, which have been made against a white background using the under-glazing technique. One of these panels is an original, while the other is a copy of the one that was taken to the Louvre Museum.

Hagia Eirene

The 1,600-year old Hagia Eirene is one of the oldest churches in the world.

Situated in the outer coutryard of Topkapı Palace, the Church of Hagia Eirene was constructed during the reign of Constantine the Great (307-337) and is the oldest church in İstanbul. Together with several other structures, this church was burned to the ground during the Nike Revolt in 532. It was reconstructed in the year 548 only to be heavily damaged as a result of earthquakes which struck in the 8th century. Emperor Constantine V had the church completely renovated and its interior decorated with mosaics and frescoes. It is known that the church was expanded during the 11th and 12th centuries. After the conquest of ‹stanbul in 1453, it was drawn into the Sultan's Walls and subsquently used as an armory and a warehouse where war booty was kept. For this reason, the church bore the name "Cebehane" and converted into a sort of weapon museum during the reign of Sultan Ahmet III (1703-1730).

It was repaired by Topkap› Field Marshall Ahmed Fethi Paşa in the year 1846 and turned into the first Turkish Museum. This building was given the name 'Müze-i Hümayun in 1869. The structure was utilized as the Military Museum starting in 1908,

Views from outside and inside the Church of Saint Irene.

whereas it was turned over to the Ministry of Culture in 1978.

The Hagia Eirene is the largest church in İstanbul after Hagia Sophia. Measuring 100 m. x 32 m., this triple nave has a basilica-like appearance and is comprised of a main space, a narthex, galleries and an atrium. The main space is divided into three naves with columns and pillars and is covered with domes and vaults. The main dome, which has 20 windows, measures 15 meters wide and 35 meters high.

There is a depiction of a cross in the abscissa. Moreover, one can see an inscription of two lines taken from the Pentateuch in the abscissa. One passes from the main space into the narthex through one of five doors and from the narthex into the atrium through one of five doors. This is the only Byzantine church found in ‹stanbul to have an atrium. The atrium is ringed with porticoes and vaulted arches, it was made narrower during the Ottoman period with the addition of a row of porticoes.

Constructed during the time of Justinian I, it is believed that the interior decoration of the church was quite ornate. However, the mosaic and frescoes have disappeared as a result of damage caused by earthquakes and other disasters. Currently open to the public as a monument/museum, Hagia Eirene is also a venue where various fine arts and cultural events are held.

A view of Saint Irene situated next to Hagia Sophia, and its environs.

PUBLICATIONS LIST

- TURKEY (Little)

- ANCIENT CIVILISATIONS OF TURKEY (Large)

- ISTANBUL (Little)

- CAPITAL OF THREE EMPIRES ISTANBUL (Large)

- TOPKAPI PALACE (Little)

- TOPKAPI PALACE (Large)

- PAMUKKALE - HIERAPOLIS (Little)

- CAPPADOCIA (Little)

- EPHESUS, KUŞADASI, PRIENE, MILET, DIDYMA

- LYCIA (Little)

- A BLUE ROMANCE (Large)

- ANTALYA (Little)

- MEVLANA AND THE MEVLANA MUSEUM (Little)

- CHORA (Little)

- TURKISH CARPET ART (Little)

- HAREM (Little)

- HAGIA SOPHIA (Little)

İlhan Akşit

İlhan Akşit was born in Denizli in 1940. After graduating as an archaeologist in 1965, he assumed a post related to the excavation of Aphrodisias. Between 1968-1976, he served as director of the Çanakkale-Troy Museum, during which time the Trojan Horse that we now see on the site was constructed.

He also directed the excavation of the Chryse Apollo Temple over a period of five years. From 1976-1978, the author acted as the director of the Underwater Archaeology Museum in Bodrum. He was appointed Director of National Palaces in 1978. During his administration, he was responsible for the restoration and reopening of many of these palaces to the public after an extended period of being closed.

In 1982 İlhan Akşit retired from his post to take up a career as an author of popular books on Turkish archaeology and tourism. He has nearly 30 titles to his credit to date, including "The Story of Troy," "Chora," "The Civilizations of Anatolia," "Istanbul," "The Blue Sailing," "The Hittites," "Cappadocia," "The Topkapı Palace," "Pamukkale," "Mustafa Kemal Atatürk," "Antalya," "Ephesus," "Lycia," "Harem," and "Turkey."